To:

_____

God sees you
through eyes of love...
and what he sees is beautiful!

From:

_____

Abiding Charity
Copyright ©2002 by Jody Houghton
ISBN 0-310-98812-8

Requests for information should be addressed to:
Inspirio, The gift group of Zondervan
Grand Rapids, Michigan 49530
http://www.inspiriogifts.com

Associate Editor and Project Manager: Janice Jacobson
Design Manager: Amy J. Wenger
Design: Kris Nelson
Editor: Molly C. Detweiler
Digital File Preparation: Donna Look

Printed in China

02 03 04/ HK / 5 4 3 2 1

ABIDING Charity

God Loves You
Just the Way You Are

Written by Jody Houghton

WITH DORIS RIKKERS

Illustrated by Jody Houghton

inspirio™

I love watching people! Waiting in airports, shopping at the mall, walking on the beach...

I'm amazed at how we all have similarities, and yet we're all so different! God made us in his own image but just look at us ... no two of us are alike! The choices we make, our sense of humor, our outlook on life, or the way we like to dress or wear our hair give zing to living.

"Shop 'til we drop"

Our differences are what make us unique. Our world would be pretty dull if we were all the same: same size, same color hair, same kind of shoes. And what if we all only liked cats, or only liked dogs? Wow, I'd miss out on loving Faith's cat, Très Jolie, and she would miss out on loving my little dog, Coco.

Let me give you another fun example. Shoes—those are the one item of clothing that really show off a person's unique style. For instance, my friend Faith loves comfortable shoes: tennis shoes and slippers are her favorites. Tennis shoes are just right for Faith, she wouldn't look like herself without them. And she has these purple slippers that are so-o-o cute! I laugh every time I think of them. Fuzzy and comfy—that's just her style! My other friend Hope loves fancy shoes, especially ones with glitter on them. She's got a special pair of shoes for every outfit and every occasion. Why she even has millennium shoes that she wore to a New Year's Eve party. Fancy shoes are just right for her. And me? My shoe preferences are pretty plain. In fact I really prefer no shoes at all.

Fancy shoes, purple slippers, or no shoes—we are all unique, different, and interesting. That's why my friends and I uniquely love each other. And that's exactly how God loves us too. He loves us for our uniqueness. He loves us just as we are. Pet preferences, fun footwear, or plain feet delight him and enhance the fact that we are all made in his image.

Finding Joy in Uniqueness

There is something exhilarating about variety. Don't you love to see a garden of flowers aglow with myriad colors, shapes and sizes? I think we achieve a full, rich beauty in life when there is variety among us; when our uniqueness is encouraged so that we have a different look from that of everyone else.

MARILYN MEBERG

I praise you,
Lord,
because I am
fearfully and
wonderfully made;
your works
are wonderful,
I know that
full well.

Psalm 139:14

Welcome to my art studio!

You're probably wondering where it is ... you don't see it do you? Well, that's because it's a place in my heart—I carry my art studio with me. All through the day designs, colors and shapes catch my eye. I see God's handiwork everywhere in his creation. I love it all so much, I just want to capture it and share it with you in my painting.

I love you lots

Charitin

With a portable art studio I can be ready to create in an instant. I set up my easel, get out the brushes, stir up the paints and prepare my canvas. Why just the other day I had this urge to paint flowers. I just love flowers with their graceful shapes, their dazzling colors. Some blossoms look like little faces to me. Their perky smiles make me grin. I like to squeeze the cheeks of snapdragons and spoon-feed them a drink of water. And the colors—every blossom has the brightest sun-yellow, orangey-orange, fantastic flaming red, or calm, clear blue. Talk about COLOR! Flowers come in every color you can imagine. Meadows are a symphony of color when filled with wildflowers.

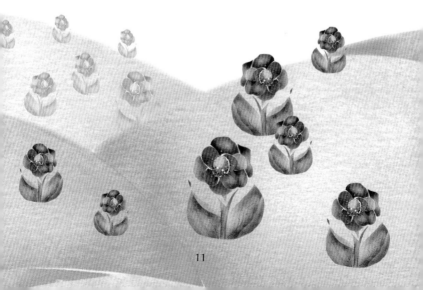

And so I love to paint flowers.

Flowers all have special meanings. Flowers are the perfect way to show how wonderful love really is. Flowers help me capture the essence of love on canvas in a new and special way.

One day after roaming through my friend Faith's garden and checking out flower gardening books from the library, I decided that instead of copying a flower, I'd create my very own, unique flower. Like no other flower before or since, this flower would capture the concept of love, celebrating the special-ness in everyone. And my uniquely created flower would have the appropriate name of

"Love-me-lots."

Of course,
the original Creator
of all things, is the
only one who can
really create a
flower. But I am ever
so thankful to him
that he has allowed
me the pleasure and
the talent to take
the colors and
shapes of his
world and paint them
for everyone I love.

If anyone
is in Christ,
he is a
new creation;
the old has gone,
the new has come!

2 Corinthians 5:17

Originality
is
simply a pair
of fresh eyes

THOMAS W.S. HIGGINSON

I love it when my friends and I all read the same book.

The discussions afterward are so exciting. Everyone picks up something different from the exact same book and the exact same story line. I'm always amazed how so many people view the same thing in so many different ways. Faith, Hope, and I all seem to relate to the story based on our own unique interests, which makes our discussion fun, yet a bit mystifying.

Faith knows what kind of flowers grow in every climate and geographic area. If a flower is mentioned in the slightest way in a novel, she loves to tell us if it likes the sun or needs shade. Last week she piped up during our discussion and said, "Did you catch the fact that the main character in this book has fresh flowers in her room all the time. See ... on page 54 it describes them? From the description and the fact that this story is set in Ireland, I bet those are ..." Faith went on to describe each flower in detail along with tips on how they should be taken care of to ensure the best blooms. I have to admit that I didn't even notice the reference to the flowers until she pointed it out!

Hope always believes that every story will turn out "happily ever after" at the end, and she has a dozen ways to solve any challenge. We are always amazed at her special outlook on life's events. We call her our "bright-eyed-shiny-person," because she sees the world through her rose-colored glasses. The other day, while we were discussing the terrible trials that the book's heroine was enduring, Hope began looking thoughtful, and then said, "This poor girl is living through a lot of difficult times, but I really, truly believe that she's going to make it through and come out really strong in the end!"

And me, well, I'm notorious for noticing the slightest "love connection." Oh, I just love it! I'll read a section of a book several times to kind of "read between the lines." This way, I can almost hear their tone of voice, see their body language, and know the intention behind their words. Faith and Hope sometimes giggle over my romantic insights, but I think it's my job to convey my point of view. Why, just yesterday I was telling them that the young man who is tending the castle's garden is so kind to our heroine … I have a feeling that true love is in the air!

When we each use our distinctive, God-given imaginations, our little book club discussions are lively and interesting. The sharing of ideas is so enriching for all of us. Each perspective reflects the uniqueness God placed in us all. This is individuality at its very best! And it's lots of fun too!

IMAGINE

Whatever is true,
whatever is noble,
whatever is right,
whatever is pure,
whatever is lovely,
whatever is admirable—
if anything is excellent
or praiseworthy—
think about
such things.

PHILIPPIANS 4:8

Imagination,
gathers up
The undiscovered
Universe,
Like jewels
in a
jasper cup.

JOHN DAVIDSON

Nine o'clock on Wednesday mornings is Swat and Giggle Tennis time!

It's just for fun and fresh air. We play round-robin style, rotating from scorekeeper to player. We work on our skills, but actually we just like to be together, wear our latest tennis outfits, and have a good chat over lunch after our court time.

Today, Faith is starting at scorekeeper. Hope and I warm up a bit and practice our serves and volleys. We each have our own style and technique. Faith's overhead shot involves a form that is so amazing: she extends her arm over her head and her mouth drops open, as if in missing the ball with her racket, she'll catch it between her teeth and blow it back over the net.

Hope's serving style always makes me giggle.

She bounces the ball in front of her—five times—then tosses the ball into the air—one, two, three times. Then she lifts her leg and gives a little hop.

All this action takes place, even before she attempts to raise the racket over her head to hit the ball.

It's her routine, her little dance. That's our Hope!

I like keeping score for our Swat and Giggle tournaments. Actually, none of us really knows how to officially keep score. However, we all know that the game starts with "love-love," or "love-all." As scorekeeper, I get to shout, "LOVE-ALL" really loudly. Everyone at the tennis club thinks I'm just saying the score, but in my own way, I'm sending more love out into the world. It's my little secret and I "love" it. The more often a player misses the ball, the more times I get to shout my favorite word, "LOVE!"

God and tennis have something in common. You don't have to do anything or earn anything, and your score will still be called LOVE!

Could we with ink the ocean fill,
And were the heavens
of parchment made,
Were every stalk on earth a quill,
And every man a scribe by trade,
To write the love of God above
Would drain the ocean dry,
Nor could the scroll
contain the whole
Though stretched from sky to sky.

CHALDEE ODE

Let us love one another,

for love comes from God.

Everyone who loves

has been born of God

and knows God

because ... God is love.

1 JOHN 4:7–8

Music has always been such a joy for my friends and me.

We love getting together for summer concerts on the courthouse lawn or gospel sing-a-longs on Sunday evenings. Tonight is a very special night of music. A new young composer is performing at the Civic Auditorium downtown. It is his night to shine. I admire his talent. He reminds me of the talents God has given all of us!

Faith, Hope, and I especially enjoy going to opening night concerts like this one. It's a Gala Affair! Although I'm usually the one who is most comfortable in my stretch pants, a t-shirt and bare feet, for this night, I'm dressing to the "nines." I'm wearing my long, black chiffon sheath, my shoulders are wrapped with my silky yellow-green scarf with the light Prussian-blue stars. I even do my hair up in very special "do."

Faith will be in her full regalia of purple and lavender. Hope loves pinks, so I'm sure she'll be wearing one of her fancy full-length, rosy numbers. For this evening, we'll look like we're heading for the Oscars in Hollywood! We always look forward to our dress-up night because it adds a bit of magic to our lives. It's our version of "Some Enchanted Evening." (I've even been caught humming that tune as we drive downtown.)

And the evening—why the evening is spectacular and the music magnificent! The special gift of music opens hearts and lifts spirits. It can calm your soul or set your toes a-tappin'. I admire the musicians and their talents, but I also realize that each person sitting in the audience, whether or not I even know them, has been given a special talent, from God to use for his honor and glory. Dressing up special and being in an auditorium with all these people reminds me that each of us is special to God.

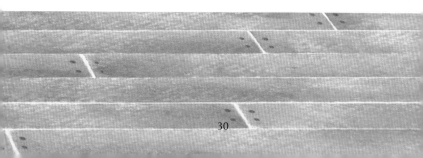

Our magical evening fills my heart with joy and renews my desire to use my God-given talents every day and in every way.

We have
different gifts,
according
to the grace
given us.

ROMANS 12:6

Your talent
is God's gift
to you.
What you
do with it
is your gift
back to God.

LEO BUSCAGLIA

It's time for my annual check up.

Everything needs maintenance; my car, oil change—every 3,000 miles, my yard—water my plants every week, and my body—a check up every year. Each year I spend the needed time to get poked and prodded in order to get the "all clear" notice from my doctor. The list includes all kinds of grams, exams, scopes, and scans.

Food Guide

This year, while sitting in the exam room

waiting for the doctor to appear, I noticed something new on the wall: A DNA chart. It was really pretty, very artistic, and so interesting. It got me thinking that each of us has our very own

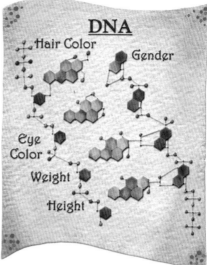

DNA—our own pattern of being. Can you believe that each of us is entirely different from everyone else? Just as no two snowflakes are alike in their pattern, so too, no two people are alike. We're uniquely and wonderfully formed by God. We are his originals. There never has been, nor will there ever be, a human being with the same combination of DNA that you or I presently have. There is only one you. There is only one me. A pure original!

My body is a one-of-a-kind container

that God has entrusted to my care. So each year when "check-up" time comes around, off I go the doctor. I am reminded to drink more water, get good rest, eat healthy food and get daily exercise. Because God loves me in such a special way, I'll make sure to take good care of me!

We are God's
workmanship,
created in
Christ Jesus
to do good works,
which God prepared
in advance
for us to do.

EPHESIANS 2:10

God's fingers
can touch nothing
but to mold it into
loveliness.

GEORGE MACDONALD

Every few years our church recruits a local photographer, and the announcement goes out, "It's time for a Photo Session." The resulting collection of color photos is gathered in a printed directory. For years afterward, everyone faithfully uses the directory to connect names from the bulletin, or from Sunday morning announcements, with smiling faces in the photos. This way we know who the morning soloist was, who just had a new baby, and what church member has accepted a Mission of Kindness or Willing-Heart Service.

This spring when it was Photo Session time, I eagerly signed up for a session for Coco and me. I talk about my little dog all the time, telling my friends about his cute little ways, so I want him in the picture with me this year. I'll get extra copies to send out with my Christmas cards too!

Photo Schedule
Choir ~ 1:30
Youth Group ~ 3:00
Charity & Coco ~ 5:00

While waiting to get our photo taken, I noticed how uncomfortable many people seemed as they sat in front of the camera; they were all fussing and fretting about how they looked. "Is my hair OK?" "Wait, I forgot my lipstick." "Is my collar straight?" "Did I blink?" "My left side is my best side."
The children, on the other hand, were a whole different story. They couldn't be more proud, with their big wide smiles, and beautiful sparkling eyes. They didn't care about their hair or collars, and as a matter of fact, they didn't want to leave, they loved the attention.

Even little Coco, with his under bite, one ear longer than the other, and tail a bit messy, proudly posed for his Church Directory photo.

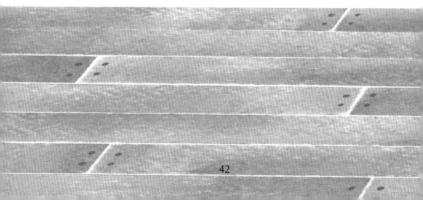

Whenever I see a happy, smiling group like those children, I know the camera has captured them at their best. Seeing people at their best is always a joy since I can see God's image radiating through each smile. God makes us in his own image. We are all precious and beautiful in His sight. So remember that and…

SMILE!

All things
bright and beautiful,
All creatures,
great and small,
All things
wise and wonderful,
The Lord God
made them all.

CECIL F. ALEXANDER

We,
who with unveiled faces
all reflect the Lord's glory,
are being transformed
into his likeness
with ever-increasing glory,
which comes from the Lord,
who is the Spirit.

2 CORINTHIANS 3:18

One day, while looking for my favorite star earrings I started looking closely at my jewelry box. It is full of treasures, not all of which would be considered "jewelry," but all are precious gems to me. They are all originals, given to me at special times in my life—birthdays, Christmas gifts, and graduations. Others are mementos puchased while on vacation. There is such a wonderful variety, all different, yet all together here in this little oak chest. If I lined up all the earrings, pins, necklaces, rings, and things, I could tell you the story of my life.

Oh, look at this, my lapel pin from the World's Fair in 1974.

What a great experience that was, seeing all the countries around the world represented at one place with all the diversity of cultures and social customs. It was a beautiful sight to behold!

Oh my, here are a few of my lavender and pink pop beads from my youth, a heart shaped locket from my high school graduation, and, oh dear, a key from my first apartment. Here's a lapis blue ring from the 70s! Oh, and here they are—my favorite gold star earrings. How long have I had these? Oh, they look great!

As I untangle gold necklaces, some fancy and expensive, some very plain, I realize that they are all priceless to me because of the treasured memories and moments they represent. Just as I treasure each piece of jewelry, no matter what its monetary worth, and thrill at the joy of finding something "lost," so too God treasures each of us.

Whether once "lost" and now found, whether 14-karat gold or electroplated silver, we are always welcomed by our creator with open loving arms. We are SPECIAL in his sight.

God loves us always as his priceless treasures!

He who counts
the stars and calls
them by their names,
is in no danger
of forgetting
His own children.

C. H. Spurgeon

How great is the love
the Father has
lavished on us,
that we should be called
children of God!
And that is what we are!

1 JOHN 3:1

My friend, Patience, is the best "doer" I know. She is the first one who will sign up to give blood, take a hot meal to someone in need, organize the bake sale, or teach Sunday school. She's on the go constantly— visiting the elderly or picking up supplies for crafts night.

But this week, Patience had to stay in bed for a few days after having minor surgery. "I want you to get plenty of rest," her doctor ordered. "The more rest you get, the faster you will recover." That was a real challenge for Patience; and her patience!

To help out, I tried to pick up where Patience left off, filling in for her at her various activities. By the end of Monday evening, I had put 100 miles on my car! First I drove to one end of town, then the other. Then I forgot the ribbon for craft night, so back to the store I went. Then I realized that I needed star stickers for the first graders' Sunday School lesson; again, back to the store I ran. I closed the week with a visit to her elderly friends at three different homes. Patience visits them every week!

At the end of that week I was so glad to be home at last! Where are my slippers and where is my chair?! I sat down for just a minute to rest and before I knew it, an hour had passed. I guess I fell asleep. I thought about my week and all the activities. It made me admire Patience for her willing heart, but it also made me thankful that we don't have to "do" anything to receive God's love. His love is a free gift. He loves us because we "are," not because we "do." All that's required is to be open to receive his gift, and here in my chair, cuddled up with my handmade quilt, I am taking time to accept and enjoy the gift of God's love!

Abiding Love

Lord, you have
created us
for yourself,
and our hearts
cannot be stilled
until they find
rest in you.

St. Augustine

In repentance
and rest
is your
salvation,
in quietness
and trust
is your strength.

"*Oh, look at your lipstick, Hope.*
And you, Faith, lavender eye shadow and long glittery eye lashes! Do you like my new foundation? It's Soft Cameo!"

While shopping at the mall, Faith, Hope, and I discovered a Make Up Make Over Fair. The sign read, "Discover the new way to smooth away those first fine lines, and view the world through bright new eyes." In just 15 minutes, the three of us were giggling with delight over our new, refreshed complexions.

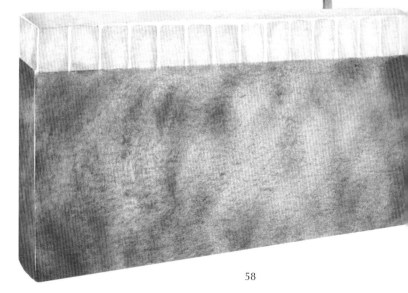

Make Up Make Over Fair

It felt so good to be pampered.

Each cosmetologist gently cleansed our faces with fluffy pink cotton balls. Then a dreamy moisturizer with vitamins A, C, and E was applied. The sweet young girl said, "It will make your skin glow—it's also Age Minimizing, you know?" The side of the bottle read, "SPF 18 to help assure a flawless future in a weightless formula that floats on your skin."

"Don't skimp on that formula," I told her, "anything *weightless* has got to be good for my *maturing* skin."

As I sat at the counter and considered the palette of foundation colors, the range of skin tones and choices available to match each person, I was amazed. The names were beautiful: Ivory, Buff, Soft Cameo, Natural Beige, Golden Honey, Sand, Light Fawn, Warm Tan, Yummy Caramel, Sweet Mocha, and Cocoa. All similar, yet all slightly different. I never knew until today that Faith is Natural Beige and Hope is glowing with the color of Golden Honey! Hope didn't notice her skin tone too much, though; she was too excited about her bright new Cherry-Raspberry lipstick and Spring Rose eye shadow!

God and all his creations, the wonder of his artistry, is endless; it takes my breath away! (And makes me feel beautiful, even without a makeover!)

Beauty is
God's handwriting.
Welcome it
in every fair face,
every fair day,
every fair flower.

CHARLES KINGSLEY

God has made
everything
beautiful
in its time.

ECCLESIASTES 3:11

Meet Charity's friends Faith & Hope

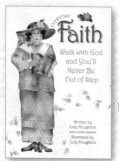

in their own
special books.
Also look
for matching
magnetic notepads
and Postcard
Daybreaks!

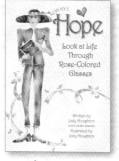

Everyday Faith
Walk with God and
You'll Never Be Out of Step
ISBN: 0-310-98570-6

Always Hope
Looking at Life Through
Rose-Colored Glasses
ISBN 0-310-98811-X

ALSO AVAILABLE:

The Forever Friends Collection
Faith, Hope, and Charity
welcome you into their circle
of friends, inspire you with
encouraging words, and tickle
your funny bone in this
delightful collection.

- Gift Book
  ISBN: 0-310-98537-4

- Postcard Daybreak™
  ISBN: 0-310-98538-2

- Magnetic Notepad
  ISBN: 0-310-98539-0

- Photo Frames
  ISBN: 0-310-98541-2
  ISBN: 0-310-98543-9
  ISBN: 0-310-98540-4

- Giftbag
  ISBN: 0-310-98483-1